How To Retire
Without Money

You Can Do It!

Dr. Noah Pranksky

TABLE OF CONTENTS

How To Retire Without Money
You Can Do It!
©Copyright 2013 by Dr. Noah Pranksky

DISCLAIMER AND TERMS OF USE AGREEMENT:
(Please Read This Before Using This Book)

Introduction – Some Food For Thought

In this book - **How To Retire Without Money:** You Can Do It! – I have relied heavily on the words of Jacob Fisker, who in my opinion is one of the best experts in the field of early retirement. I have included the resources he cites to better serve my readers in completely understanding that this topic is a serious one and very much attainable…truly you can do it!

This will probably come as a shocker to most people: Three economists from leading universities have found that "a substantial fraction of persons die with virtually no financial assets -- 46.1% with less than $10,000 -- and many of these households also have no housing wealth and rely almost entirely on Social Security benefits for support." Got that?

The findings, in a paper published by the National Bureau of Economic Research show that a huge portion of America is relying almost completely on Social Security, and that they die with hardly any money to their name.

I wrote this book because of the facts cited above. I have been a research behavioral science doctor for over 31-years. I decided to use my research abilities and attempt to discover "How To Retire Without Money".

Dying broke is a very good thing from the standpoint that you not only screw the government on your way out but in reality you can't take it with you and where you going they don't use money.

Furthermore, the professors' data above reflects millions of Americans not living perfect financial lives, but instead struggling to get by in retirement. They don't end up running out of assets on their last day, but long before it.

So let's put it in perspective...the average monthly Social Security benefit is $1,230. That's $14,760 per year. Can you imagine yourself living on that – or, let's even up it a little, on, say, $20,000 or $25,000 per year?

And would you want to?

The experts suggest that when it comes time to live off your nest egg, you should plan to withdraw about 4% of it in the first year, and then adjust for inflation annually. Thus, if you're looking for income of $40,000 per year, you'll need a million dollars. (Remember that everyone's needs are different -- you might want more income than that, but you might also be expecting some Social Security income and perhaps even some pension money to make up some of that income.)

If you're reading this wishing you'd started saving for retirement aggressively many years ago, don't freak out. All is not lost, no matter how imperfect your current financial situation may seem. There is still a bunch of ways that you can make your retirement much more comfortable. Here are some of the main ones:

• **Aggressive savings.** The old rule of thumb to sock away 10% of your income is too low for many people. Aim for 15%, or even 20% or more, if you can. And remember that due to the ability of money to grow over time, the dollars you sock away today will likely contribute much more to your retirement than dollars you sock away next year or in five years. So don't put it off.

• **Effective Investing.** Keeping everything in a bank account isn't investing -- with interest rates below the average rate of inflation; you're actually losing buying power every year. Bonds are appropriate for those in or near retirement, but ideally in combination with stocks, which usually build wealth much faster. Within the stock world, you needn't take chances on obscure potential high-fliers, either. Over long periods, healthy, growing dividends can build great wealth. And if all goes well, the dividend payouts will rise over time, as will the stock prices, too.

• **Retire later**. The benefits are many: For each extra year you work, you'll keep workplace benefits such as health-care coverage, and won't have to pay for them. You'll also delay tapping your nest egg for money to live off. And ideally, you'll be able to contribute to the nest egg for a few more years, as well. Meanwhile, for every year that you delay starting to receive Social Security benefits, they'll go up about 8%. Delay three years, and you'll collect roughly 24% more. That's a big difference!

• **Cost Cutting Works - Downsize.** Another way to make your retirement fund last longer is to use less of it each year. You might move into a smaller house, for example, or to a region with a lower cost of living. You and your partner might make do with one car in retirement, instead of two, saving money on insurance and upkeep. And if you've been supporting some grown and able children or grandchildren, you might rein in that spending, too.

Some or all of these moves can have a powerful effect on your financial condition now and in retirement. You don't have to be among the 46% who die with more worries than dollars.

Okay, now to the good stuff...

Chapter 1 – How Much Money Can You Live On Each Year?

In my Introduction, I said the following: *"So let's put it in perspective...the average monthly Social Security benefit is $1,230. That's $14,760 per year. Can you imagine yourself living on that – or, let's even up it a little, on, say, $20,000 or $25,000 per year? And would you want to?"*

Here is an interesting take on this exact same subject (be advised I have edited this for easier reading):

http://earlyretirementextreme.com/how-i-live-on-7000-per-year.html

How I live on $7,000 per year
Published on October 10th, 2011
Posted by Jacob in Early Retirement, Finance, Work

If you're new here, this blog will give you the tools to become financially independent in 5 years. Here's how I did it (this can be seen in Chapter 2) and here are a few dozen online journals from other people who are currently doing it.

http://forum.earlyretirementextreme.com/forum.php?id=9

This is not some stupid get rich quick scheme. The method is robust and replicable (no need to win the lottery, sell your business, or win at real estate), but not easy; much in the same way that a diet results in weight loss but is hard to follow persistently unless you set your mind to it.

The key is to save 75%+ of your net income and invest it in income producing assets (bonds and dividend stocks). This is done by running your personal finances much like a business, thinking about assets and inventory and focusing on efficiency and value for money.

Also, check out my answers to Frequently Asked Questions which also covers common misconceptions regarding my personal budget, blog income, retirement, marriage, children, health care, etc (Read these in Chapter 3).

Disclaimer: This post has gotten wildly popular on the internet so in many cases this post is the first and only post many people will read. Regular readers will already know that I'm married and that we split expenses 50/50. Hence, our combined budget is $14,000/year. For first time readers, let me point out that I have, however, been living on $7,000/year or less for at least a decade and I've only been married for 5 of those years. Getting married meant saving money on things like rent, but it also meant having to compromise and spending money on things which I rarely use and otherwise wouldn't have bought myself. Speaking in terms of budgets, it's been a wash. I spend as much being single as being married.

Okay, that does it. I'm getting tired of the pervasive media articles that detail how people are "surviving" or "barely managing" on what qualifies as average or definitely median household incomes. This is like writing a articles about 5'10" guys who are "struggling" with their height issues complete with tips and tricks on how to cope with their shortage. Ha! For the record, 5'10" is the average height of a US male. Fun fact:

This is also the median, since there are few 12′ tall guys to skew the distribution.

The waterfall that finally crushed the camel was a Yahoo article which discusses how a single person ~~"survives"~~ is living well on $20,000/year, but that's just one out of many. In particular, it followed an initial article on how a family survives on $40,000/year. This is pretty close to the median household income in the US! It means that about half of everybody, that's 150+ million people, is currently living on LESS than those amounts. Surely, that's no secret, and surely that's not very remarkable either.

Then there is the article of a family that's struggling on $250,000/year. Poor guys! They spend more on cleaning services than I do on pretty much everything combined. Regardless of how much I made, I think I would pick up a goddamn broom myself before I started talking about my financial struggles. The gall!

The media must be living in a bubble that is entirely separated from Main Street. Look, it isn't that hard to find someone who lives on $10,000/year, or $5,000/year. I can even provide a couple of pointers to people who live on $0/year. (And no, they're not living under a bridge).

The problem is, and I think I get it now, is that the media is in the business of pushing content in order to sell ads, so they must write for the biggest common denominator. It makes strategic sense for a magazine to write articles about families who spend $48,000 per year and now struggle because they had to cancel their Netflix subscription. Or for a magazine to write articles about families who spend a quarter million per year and now struggle because they had to give up their daily fireworks. People can sympathize with people who are similar to themselves and the entitlement-class always thinks they're hard done to. So okay media, you are forgiven.

However, I still have a problem with the numbers. Back in the days when I started this blog, I made the mistake of calling it Early Retirement Extreme. The first problem was the word retirement which means different things to different people (see FAQs in Chapter 3). The second problem, which is relevant here, is the word extreme.

I get many comments from so-called "complainypants" that I'm too "extreme". The extremeness seems to revolve around lentils and the low amount of money I spend, about $7,000/year.

Let's make another attempt of dealing with the lentil issue. (Please bear with me, it frustrates me because some people will read some post I wrote about lentils and discard the ideas of early financial independence outright without a second thought because they don't like lentils. That is a sad loss of potential and all because this author likes lentils.) Now, somewhere on this blog I discuss the fact that I used to eat lentils in grad school because it was quick and easy to cook. Consequentially, some now think that's all I've been eating for the past 15 years. This is not the case (see below). I suspect if I had said I used to eat ramen as an undergraduate, people would understand perfectly. But noooo...I ate lentils so I'm weird. Anyway ...

The second and more important aspect is the $7,000/year. The Wheaton Eco-scale (see this at the end of Chapter 3) explains this in a brilliant way. Consider people living at different budgets, e.g. $100k, $80k, $60k, $50k, $40k, $30k $20k, $15k, $10k, $7.5k, $5k, $2.5, $1k, and $0k. Now, what Wheaton observes is that people who spend one or two levels below you are inspiring to you in terms of budget reductions. People who spend three levels below you are slightly nutty and people who spend four or more levels below your level are crazy or downright extreme. This holds no matter where you are. If you spend 60k, then 50k and 40k is inspiring, 30k is nutty and 20k is crazy. If you spend 30k, then 20k and 15k is inspiring, 10k is nutty, and 7.5k is crazy. Conversely, people who spend a couple of levels above you are considered prodigal and wasteful.

The problem is that budgets denominated in dollars are very one-dimensional. If you look at the article above of a guy who spends 20k/year—that's almost three times as much as I do—while living in the same area (San Francisco bay area), I note that he does something I don't (go to bars) but I have something he hasn't (health insurance). Otherwise we have and do many of the same things.

What is the difference? If I had to venture a guess, I'd say I'm more frugal (the way your grandparents were frugal—in fact what I do wouldn't be considered very extreme by your grandparents or great grandparents—I'd probably be average from their perspective) and I adhere more to a do-it-your-self ethics. I'd also suspect that I've solved the housing situation better. On the other hand, he doesn't have a car (but in San Francisco, that would be normal).

What really is remarkable is the similarity in lifestyle despite the disparity in spending.

I really hope that this is empathetically understood, especially by those who say they're "not willing to be as extreme as me"—someone who spends 15-20k would be a typical example. What I hear is essentially that they're not willing to learn how to stretch their dollars further. They're saying that they're not willing to get the same thing that I have for $500/month instead of the $1400/month they're paying. They're not willing to learn or to think beyond their current frame of mind.

To be clear, the ERE efficiency strategy will get you a $20k lifestyle (if you're single) or a $40k lifestyle (which is the median for a US family) for much less money down. Why wouldn't anyone want that? Just about the only ones I can think of who doesn't want that are the corporations that prey on consumerists.

I'm sorry, but I find this to be the most frustrating part about this blog or the ERE project as a whole. I may just be a very bad salesman.

Now, just for fun, I'll answer the same questions as the ones in the article above. Contrast and compare in the comments.

Note: You can find a breakdown of my $7,000 budget in the frequently asked questions (Chapter 3). I have been living on $5-7,000/year for about a decade now. This includes 5 years as a single and 5 years being married.

Do you avoid a lot of the expenses that many of your peers spend money on, such as technology and meals out?

I would think so. I usually go to the mall to perform a kind of an anthropological expedition once a year and I see nothing there which interests me. Really nothing. It's mostly mid-range consumer stuff which will tragically end up in a garage or a landfill about ten years down the road. Except for the rare pick-up pizza, we do not get our meals out, mostly because I hate eating out. My wife cooks practically all of our meals. However, we do have many of the same things. We have internet, Netflix, and a car (my wife drives it; I paid for half of its price and half of its operational cost in exchange for occasional rides). My computer is a seven year old 12" PowerBooks.

What's your typical meal?

A very typical meal would be a salad from the garden (cucumber, tomato, lettuce, mesclun) with homemade thousand island dressing (vinegar+ketchup+mayonnaise, just try it, that's all there is to it) followed with pasta with a sauce based on beans, canned tomatoes, zucchini from the garden, onions, and olives. I douse this with hot sauce. For some strange reason, I'm famous for eating lentils. I did that when I was in grad school because it's quick and easy but since my wife took over the cooking and I took over the dishes and laundry about seven years ago, this doesn't happen anymore.

What about clothes?

Practically never, by which I mean maybe once a year (usually socks and underwear). In the winter, I usually wear a suit+jacket and a Hawaiian shirt (can you tell, I got style) or even a dress shirt. I also have a pair of jeans and a couple of "participation" t-shirts. In the summer I wear a pair of white Dockers shorts. A lot of my clothes (I don't have a lot) are 10+ years old. The reason it lasts that long is that I line dry it. I will also wear clothes until it fails catastrophically (rips). I'm not opposed to Goodwill and Salvation Army, but usually they don't have my size of pants, 33×34; sweaters and jackets last decades (my current one is almost 20 years old); and t-shirts are incidental.

What about going on dates?

We're both homebodies. When we first met, my wife's friends dragged us out to a karaoke bar. We left after an hour and ended up back at my place—less noise, easier to talk. Our dates consisted of home cooked dinners. These days I suppose our dates consists of walking the dog.

Do you indulge in any luxuries?

A lot of my stuff falls in the luxury category. For instance, the suit mentioned above is a $500 suit (I bought it on sale for $100). This may sound expensive until you realize that the suit is old and thus it holds up rather well. The amortization rate that is, spreading the cost out over the years comes to very little. When I buy tools or other things to enjoy, I buy near the top (this is why the Mall doesn't work for me). For example, I've acquired several $300 hand planes for my woodworking. This may also sound expensive, but realize that if I ever tire of wood working, I can sell those for close to what I paid for them. This makes them much cheaper than a $45 hand plane from the big box store. In fact, many of my hobbies are financed by selling my old gadgets. My one exception is my martial arts training. I spend over $1,000 per year on that or almost 15% of my entire budget.

Do you have health insurance?

I do. I have a high-deductible health plan and a health savings account (for the tax deduction). You can read more about it in my post on how to find cheap health insurance without the need for an employer (something Americans have to worry about. See Chapter 4).

Do you have any savings for emergencies?

What, do you mean if I suddenly needed to raise $100,000 in cash because there was a sale on real estate? Sure, I do.

Do you anticipate or look forward to having a higher salary one day?

I'm financially independent. To me more money and higher incomes are more of a way of keeping score in the rat race and I left that race. Sure, I would like to have more money, because I like money and having more of it is nicer. I don't find it worth the sacrifice and I only consider it incidental to the things I do or that I'd be willing to engage in. I would say in some respects, money does serve as a proxy for value. For instance, if we consider my book sales, I'm more pleased by the fact that people are willing to pay $10 to read my ideas than I am at receiving the royalties. I've been asked why I didn't keep working in order to have more stuff or more "financial security" (I would have been a millionaire at 38 if I hadn't retired at 33). However, I already have all the stuff I would possible want to spend my time taking care of (I don't like dusting and organizing stuff), and beyond a certain net worth, more net worth does not protect you financially. In other words, if there's an event (like hyperinflation) that could cause you to lose one million dollars, it could just as easily cost you five million dollars.

What about retirement–do you plan on ever saving enough to retire?

Already did it. If one is frugal and don't make the mistake of buying the two financial independence killers on credit, that would be "more house than you need" and "more car than you need", and pay a little extra instead of the "buy and throw away" merchandise in the mall, even an average salary (which I had) will allow a person to become financially independent at a rather young age. You don't need a six figure salary to pull it off.

Do you have any advice to others trying to live on $7,000 a year?

Yes, read this blog or just ask your grandparents. $7,000 for one person, which translates into ~ $14,000 for our two person household (which is located in a city with a cost of living index of 131), seems extreme today, but if you go back 50 years and compare how people lived back then, it isn't all that impressive. Furthermore, by many accounts people were happier back then. They weren't zooming around trying to buy the newest cell phone model or waiting for the waiters in order to eat, and stressing out about their resumes in order to keep living their leveraged and amped up lifestyles—if you call that living. Okay, I rant, but from my perspective, my lifestyle is the sane choice, and it's everybody else who's extreme.

Chapter 2 – How One person Retired on $7,000 PER YEAR.

http://earlyretirementextreme.com/how-i-live-on-7000-per-year.html

This was one of the first blog posts I wrote when I started this site back in 2007. It is also one of the most popular. I describes what I did in the period from 2001–2006. Maybe someday I'll write a summary of the period 2007–2011, but for now you'll have to dig into the blog to see what has changed and what has remained the same. When I set out on this journey in 2001, I didn't have anyone to follow or look to for ideas. Blogs didn't really exist and I didn't have access to a good library, so I had to figure out most things myself. In retrospect and with more guidance I would have done it differently and with less personal hassle. So don't think you have to follow the details of what I did to reach a similar goal. In fact, you can follow the journals of some of my readers to see how it's done better than I did. With that in mind, here's my story …

I posit that most people can attain financial independence in less than 10 years and in less than 5 if they are truly determined. I also submit that many people are not willing to make the necessary changes.

My journey towards financial independence was not always with financial independence in mind per se. Had that been my sole goal all a long I would have done things differently and probably faster e.g. 3-4 years instead of 5. If I had a six figure income, which I never had, I would be able to do it in 2 or 3 years. However, that's the thing. As we gain in knowledge and wisdom our priorities change as that which was once important becomes less important as things are put in a different and hopefully bigger perspective.

First of all I have to confess that I have never been dumb with money. I believe I once made an accidental overdraft because I forgot about an automatic payment, but otherwise I have never been in the red zone. I also suspect I was born with certain miserly qualities so that I did not need to change my basic personality too much. Spending money on "spontaneous fun" e.g. perishables like candy, ice cream, parties, beer, going out... have never meant much to me. Instead I was more interested in gadgets and electronics. Basically I would discover some new hobby. Then I would save until I had the money, and then I would go out and buy a new computer, then a SLR camera, then a HiFi rack, then another computer, then a telescope, etc. Since I enjoyed gadgets a lot more than sugar, alcohol, cab fares and other things that seem to make everybody else happy, I was already ready to save for big items and thus it was not so hard for me to aim for something bigger.

The first thing I realized was therefore that my expensive hobbies had to go and be replaced with "free" hobbies, which meant no more buying toys. Instead I become interested in system administration, Linux, and geopolitics, in particular resource depletion and overpopulation – which of course makes for great ice breakers at any cocktail party. I did not immediately make the connection to think of hobbies that make me money. At the time when I started saving money to keep it rather than spend it on the next big piece of electronics, I was a grad student living in a dorm room. There were 18 other people on the floor and we all shared the kitchen, 3 showers and 3 toilets. Most grad students I have known all had their own apartment, their own car, etc. and thus leave school with a degree and a ton of student debt. I did, however, not live there to save money but to meet other people more easily. In addition it was only a 10 minute walk (or a 5 minute run) from my office and 5 minutes from the closest supermarket. Thus I did not need a car or a bike.

The two personal finance books that have influenced and inspired me the most and which I caught hold of at that time was Rich Dad Poor Dad and Your money or your life. If I could have only two personal finance books those would be it!

Your money or your life can easily be summarized. There are two main ideas. The first idea is to calculate your real wage by subtracting taxes, transport, business clothes, cost of living (for instantly, suppose your job requires you to live in New York City), and dividing by time spent on the job, time spent on commuting, and time spent unofficially preparing yourself for your job. If you do this calculation you might find some particularly scary numbers. For instance, the hourly real wage of a commuting grad student (e.g. a highly skilled and competent person who would fetch $40-60k in the private sector) is certainly below the minimum wage. The second idea is to use the real wage to calculate the cost of something in hours. Suppose a Wii is $400 and your real wage comes to around $8/hr. Then you would have to work for 50 hours to get it. Since we only live once and never get this time back, those 50 hours have to be weighed against the game system. 50 hours seems fair to me, however, there was no way I was going to add 10 more hours on top of that by buying it on credit. In particular, I did not want to pay for my house 3 times over by getting a mortgage. Thus my initial motivation was to save for a house to avoid the mortgage interest.

Apparently the personal finance blogging community doesn't like Rich Dad Poor Dad because it does not contain enough "actionable" items and/or because the author gave some questionable real estate advice in some of his subsequent seminars. For me, though, that book was like striking gold. It completely changed my attitude towards money from being something one spends to buy stuff to being something one invests to make more money. Leave it to me to figure out the details, I am a smart guy, but it takes a genius to create a paradigm shift and I am not a genius.

By Rich Dad Poor Dad standards I was still thinking like a poor person, saving and paying in cash and I was probably on my way to thinking like a middle class person who buys everything on credit. Instead I started thinking like a wealthy person and having my money work for me while cutting down on my liabilities and avoiding having me work for money. My guess is that it is probably easier to go from poor to wealthy than from middle class to wealthy. The middle class is weighed down by a large set of liabilities in the form of house payments, car payments, credit payments, educational payments, ... Once you have those liabilities, they are very hard to give up to replace with assets.

Initially I was just putting my money in savings accounts and watching it grow. In retrospect pure savings accounts turned out to be a good idea, since that was the period of 2001-2004 which was mostly a bear market. But an important point is that I did not invest for the first 3 years out of the 5 years it took me to gain financial independence. For extreme savers, financial independence is not achieved through investing. There is simply not enough time for compounding to make much of a difference. Instead compounding becomes somewhat irrelevant as the eventual portfolio becomes more focused on preserving principal, generating income, and not suffering too much in terms of inflation and taxes.

One thing I noticed early on was that small expenditures could quickly add up. $100 there, $50 there, $5 every day for a month. In the months where I bought very little my savings seemed to go up very fast. If I spent more my savings would go up less. It isn't rocket science that sweating the small stuff IS important. Therefore I canceled my radio subscription and eventually my gym membership. Of course it goes without saying that I did not have a TV. I did have a cheap internet connection though. I stopped shopping for clothes outside of thrift stores. I also changed my diet into what was basically two different types of meals for dinner for which I could cook up a 6 day supply in 30 minutes: Lentil soup and tuna salad(*). For breakfast I had oatmeal with water, seeds and raisins, and for lunch I ate a couple of bananas. Maybe once a week, I would buy more interesting things (spices are my friends). Of course when I went home to visit, eating different food was quite a joy, but it is not that difficult to eat the same kind of healthy food day after day. It only takes a little getting used to. A large part of the world eats nothing but rice and while it is hard in the beginning one quickly gets used to thinking of food as fuel for the body rather than snacking entertainment.

(*) You don't need to eat this boring. This strategy was mainly due to me being in grad school and not wanting to spend very much time cooking. Many grad schools rely on ramen because of the time pressure.

One year I believe I only bought three new books. My savings rate of my after tax wage income was pushing 80% that year. However, that was so boring that I vowed not to skimp on things that somehow improves me i.e. makes me smarter or in better shape. I think that is a good rule to go by even though it pushed the rate down to 70%. I think one can get too extreme. Today I allow myself more "frivolous" expenditures thanks to my substantial passive income. We even have cable now.

Still my savings rate on my after tax wage income is around 40% which my passive income bumps up to almost 80%. The main reason for that is that since I think a lot about my purchases, I simply don't need to spend a lot of money to be comfortable.

Financial independence is only one form of independence. I was interested in other forms of independence as well. After all, what do you do if people won't take your money or your money becomes worthless or you lose it all? Therefore I experimented with simplified cooking, raw eating, solar ovens, and growing my own vegetables (not a success). I also tried to make things last longer. I mended socks, repaired electronics, etc. Most of the times I found that I could do without something or jerry rig a simpler solution without heading down to the store. It may seem like trivial example but rather than buying an energy saving gadget, I simply got used to switching things off manually when I didn't use them. Simple to understand but the difference in attitude is huge and results follow when this attitude is taken to other levels as well. For instance, how would I deal with 90F heat? I could buy an AC unit, buy a fan, or I could simply learn how to sweat. Sweating may sound uncomfortable, but after a while the body adapts and the heat is no longer an issue.

It is only when you live in an air conditioned society that you never get a chance to adapt always being subjected to the bad effects of going between hot and cool and consequently adopt the preconception that it is impossible to live without AC. Well, people managed to live without AC less than a hundred years ago. The same goes for heating. Even though the heating was included in the rent where I lived, I experimented one winter with whether I could do without heating in a temperate climate. This meant long underwear and sleeping in a thick bathrobe under a sheet, a fleece blanket and a sleeping bag, but I managed just fine. Today I am comfortable in a t-shirt down to 65F relying on a larger than average metabolism from a vigorous exercise plan. This in turn means that I can eat well and maintain a single digit body fat percentage. It all fits together.

I began simplifying my lifestyle trying to rely more on skills and adaption to the environment rather than on tools (think money). I have researched this with a fairly open mind. I have looked into car-living or boat-living, places where every cubic inch of space counts to get ideas for how to maximize my use of space and thus minimize my need for space. I know a thing or two about homesteading from researching in how to be creative in making solutions from scratch. I know how to make soap from scratch (though it's easier to buy) and what common household items to substitute for shampoo or toothpaste. I even know how to make baking soda! I can cook with almost no heat and very few utensils. There are of course a lot of "actionable" details to this story, but in trying to convey the idea to other people the biggest obstacle has generally been the frame of mind rather than things to do.

We have become so used to heading down to the store and thinking that we need everything we can buy there! It is a lot easier to learn techniques than it is to change one's entire belief system of how the world hangs together. The end result of all this was to make everything I truly needed to live well fit into a couple of large suitcases and reduce my expenditures to what is considered somewhat below the poverty level while maintaining a comfortable lifestyle. In terms of quality I live somewhat above the ordinary consumer class standard of living since I own more luxury items but in terms of quantity my life style is quite a bit below.

When I finally got my PhD, I had no student debt. Furthermore I had saved enough of my grant/paychecks to actually make up half of my current net worth! After finishing my PhD, I became an academic researcher and was now making about as much as a state trooper or a long haul trucker. As I have hinted in earlier posts, I did not become financially independent by having a six figure income. Far from it. Rather it was through creative ways of increasing my savings by being increasingly more independent of the general economy. Quite an adventure.

I think it has been argued before whether a college education is really worth it. My answer is that it depends. A college education is certainly not a magic bullet to financial success. Monetarily, a college education and a tradeable skill are probably equally valuable, since going without a college education means earning money sooner and not accruing any student debts. What is important is money handling skills, not income. On the other hand, although I could have had a much higher income by NOT getting a PhD (entering grad school is almost financial suicide) and choosing engineering or accounting rather than science (that's a specific as I am going to get), I did not think of expected income or even employability when I picked my major. However, unlike the higher income educations, my particular major has allowed to visit more than 10 countries for conferences and workshops without paying a dime out of my own pocket, publish many articles and part of a book as well advise on million dollar projects and thus have some influence in the scientific world. Having a "blue collar" job would probably not have been as intellectually satisfying to me, but that's just me. For those who have their heads and hands screwed on right, spending up to 10 years in the educational system just to learn how to research arcane details that are interesting to maybe only 5 or 10 people in the world probably sounds crazy as well whereas building a beautiful house is a great accomplishment.

Having just graduated with a PhD and paired everything I could possibly need into a couple of large suitcases (except for my humongous book collection) I moved to my new job. With everything in a couple of suitcases it is quite easy to move. It takes maybe a couple of hours to pack and clean the place and off you go. I had also made sure not to exceed the airline weight limit for either suitcase to get the added freedom of flying with my stuff and not paying for excess weight.

Prior to my arrival I had decided that after 4 years of sharing a kitchen and bathroom with 18 other people, I wanted the luxury my own kitchen and my own bathroom. Luckily I found such a room on the top floor of a house which the landlord rented out to visiting students and researchers. This was within walking distance of my new job, so I was good to go. Groceries were acquired during lunch breaks by hauling a messenger bag over to the nearest supermarket which unfortunately was in the opposite direction. I kept eating like I used to.

One problem was that I hadn't moved my bank accounts, so after a week of eating out with my new boss, etc. I was down to a couple of cans of tuna, a large bag of rice, and some soy sauce for the second week until I got my pay check. I suppose I could have gotten a payday loan, but I was used to eating simple, so eating rice three times a day for a couple of days was no big deal. After all most of the world does just that. Shortly after that I got the bank connections in order, but I did learn an important lesson. It does not matter how much money you have, if you cannot buy food. Second, if you can rough it a little, you have choices e.g. I could attend to the social arrangements for my new job (the cost of having a job) even though I didn't really have money to eat.

It was shortly thereafter that I met DW who in addition turned out to work just a couple of buildings over from where I worked. After the incident at the karaoke bar dating comprised mostly hanging out at either her place or my place. After several months of dating like that we decided that we might as well move in together. After having looked around, we found a nice little house for rent within walking distance of our work. In my case walking distance usually means less than 4 miles but this house was less than 2 miles away, had a huge backyard and was located in a quiet neighborhood just at the edge of the city. Nice! At $660 a month it was hard to beat (except for the $400 apartment we found later just before we moved to CA). Of course since the house had been empty for a couple of years prior everything and I do mean everything started failing in short succession just after we moved in. The nice thing about renting though is that the landlord is usually responsible for maintaining the appliances.

DW was used to eating more varied than I was, so I gave up my lazy Spartan diet figuring that I could afford the luxury given that I now had a real job. Besides, not eating lentil soup 6 days a week interspersed with tuna sandwiches anymore seemed to be worth the $70 increase in food expenditures. I mean, in 30 years, I might not have any taste buds left to appreciate the $700 of monthly food money that this increase would compound into.

We got most of our furniture used. Some of it was donated from people at our workplace moving on to better things. Other things we bought used. We also bought a few crappy particle board pieces new. You generally get what you pay for unless you buy used. In that case you tend to get a lot more than what you pay for. When we moved, we freecycled a lot of our furniture, sold other furniture. On a net basis I don't think we paid anything for the furniture that did not come with us. Buying used often means that depreciation costs are fully factored in, so effectively, we got free use of a lot of that furniture.

Being normal, DW had a car even though we lived, worked, and shopped practically the same places even before we met. It's been a subject of continuous debate ever since whether to keep it or not. One thing I noted was that I could get from our house to my office in 30 minutes by walking. Going by car, I could get there in about 20 minutes. Running I could get there in 10 minutes. Thus often I would simply take off on foot before DW got the car defrosted, etc. and we would arrive at the same time. Eventually I bought a used bike for $35 from a professor that was leaving for California. I ran that bike into the ground but it was worth it given that I could make the trip in 10 minutes instead of 30 minutes. Of course the bike was useless during winters. Sometimes I would brave the cold (-17F) and walk through the snow which was conveniently thrown onto the sidewalk. Walking was passively discouraged in the city we lived in. One might say the citizens were not particularly enlightened.

One resident explained to me that the reason that there weren't any more sidewalks was because the voters believed that sidewalks would provide poor people with an easy way of getting around. Yes and? Well, clearly poor people that otherwise could not afford a car are mostly criminals. Huh? Read that one again, if that did not make sense the first time. It still doesn't make a whole lot of sense to me, but I guess there was something to it as I once got held up by a campus police cruiser (spot light in my face and the loud voices from a conversation at 30 feet – I could not see a thing) while walking home from work. He probably thought I was casing the bank I just walked by, but I eventually managed to convince him that that was my standard route for walking to and from my job. Next day I got a ride from him while walking to work. He was probably trying to make up for the episode the night before. I also got well intended albeit naive advice from people I passed on the campus parking lot ranging from how I should dress for the weather to questions from strangers about where I got the nice gear? So I kept walking although I must admit that I did get a ride from DW when the weather was particularly bad or when I was particularly lazy.

Meanwhile savings kept going up, but at this point I was starting to think about investments.

Chapter 3 – Frequently Asked Questions (FAQs)

http://earlyretirementextreme.com/frequently-asked-questions

Q: I find it hard to believe that you/anyone can live on $5-7k/year [without living in hardship].
A: That's alright; I find it hard to believe how you/anyone can spend $30,000/year [without flushing money down the drain]. A simple break-down of the most important expenses (in year 2011) would be $270/month for my half of the rent+utilities; $95/month for health insurance; $75-100/month for food; $95/month for martial arts; $50/month for my half of the car; $50/month for my half of the dog; $20/month for internet. My other expenses are negligible. The car, dog, and the gym are more recent optional splurges which I've added as my portfolio has increased. So my core expenses are $5,820/year and my optional expenses are $2,340/year almost half of which is spent on martial arts. Take away the martial arts and it comes to $7,020/year. Also keep in mind that we currently live in one of the most expensive areas of the country (San Francisco Bay area) which has a cost of living index of 131 relative to the average US city of 100. My wife spends a similar amount per year.

Q: I think 30 is way too young to be retired!

A: Could it be that you're stuck in the conventional "school-career-retire-die" way of thinking about life? If so, you need to read a bit more of this site because that's NOT the kind of retirement ERE is about. Here retirement is used in the "becoming financially independent and using that freedom to pursue other interests"-sense. Incidentally, this is not a new idea. Rather it is an old and somewhat forgotten idea. If you read biographies of people like Ben Franklin or Joseph Conrad, you will often see that they "retired" from one profession to take up another interest. Being financially independent and also well-rounded and possessing more than one skill made that possible.

Q: What's your net worth?
A: Somewhat more than 4060 times of what I spend annually. This will theoretically last the rest of my life with a very high safety margin. If you don't understand why investing the equivalent of 40+ years of expenses will last longer than 40 years, you need to read up on some basic retirement math or ask a CFP or similar.

Q: Do you clip coupons?
A: No. Coupons are mostly for preprocessed foods and poor goods that aren't selling well. Cooking from staples is less expensive and requires less time if you consider the flexibility and the time saved from clipping and going to multiple stores. Good stuff does not need coupons to sell and staples are like commodities: You can't brand name potatoes or lettuce. More generally speaking, I would say I am in a different class of frugal. I am not frugal because I need to cut cash outlays. I can plunk down $5000 easily. Now, if I can pay $5000 for something and sell it in five years for $4800, I have only spent $40 a year compared to buying something for $600 with a $100 rebate and having to throw it out 5 years later. This is how I save money.

Q: Do you dumpster-dive for food?

A: No, I'm not sure where that one came from. The only thing I've ever pulled out of a dumpster was some newspapers from the recycling bin to feed my composting worms.

Q: Do you make your own soap?
A: No, I'm not sure where that one came from either, but manufactured soap is one of the wonders of industrialization. It is much easier to buy than it is to make—when I talk about "making soap", I mean rendering it from lye and lard, not melting and reforming existing soap into cuter shapes. On the other hand I do make my own laundry detergent (out of borax, soap, and washing soda).

Q: How much did you pay for your degree?
A: I didn't pay anything because I grew up in Denmark where advanced education was/is free insofar you have the required grade point average. If I had grown up in the US I would probably have done the stupid thing and get into student debt because I was still ignorant about money when I was 18. In hindsight, that is, knowing what I know now... and what I'm telling you... I would have either gone to a state university and paid rent to my parents to get a degree in a skilled profession (engineering, accounting) or gone to a community college and gotten a degree in a skilled trade. I think the latter is much underrated. This is probably because universities have more money available for advertising than do community colleges even though if you are equally ambitious you will be making as much money with a trade as you will in a profession.

Q: How can you possibly pay for health insurance on a total budget of $500/month? I pay $500 per month on health insurance alone, so your budget does not make sense. [Most common question on the blog]
A: Your health insurance is probably "fully loaded". I pay $69 each month (2008) for a high deductible health plan which I obtained on the free market, that is, no "corporatist cheating" of having to get it through a job or a family member's job. In fact, I think tax laws favoring employer sponsored group insurance is grossly unjust!

I max out my HSA which reduces my taxes by $450 a year (I'm in the 15% bracket). My net costs of health insurance are thus $402 per year. Back when I was in the 25% tax bracket making my net cost $69*12-0.25*2900 = $103/year. How do you like them apples?

When I was working I intentionally dumped my company health insurance for the HDHP—note that many companies only offer the fully loaded plans. Ask your employer if they offer a HDHP. In such cases it is not unusual that employers would cover you for free.

HDHP's are cheap because most of the responsibility is on the consumer. They remain cheap too. For example, when I am 55 years old, the cost will be $155 per month in today's dollars. It should also be noted that I don't have any pre-existing conditions and that I take a more conservative (continental) approach to health care, that is, I believe in prevention rather than treating symptoms and I don't medicate for everything. DW has her health insurance through her company, so we have separate health insurances.

Q: What about dental or vision?
A: I don't have dental or vision insurance. Paying insurance that covers "regular maintenance" like teeth cleaning or contact lenses which these kinds of insurance do makes no sense whatsoever. Suppose everybody pays $25/month for contacts. Now do you think that everybody paying that $25 through an insurance company will make it any cheaper? No, the insurance company will add a $5 administrative fee—they most definitely will not give away free money. As such this kind of insurance is nothing but a financing plan for people who can't figure out how to save the money for a $200 dental visit. The point of insurance is to cover rare events with a six-figure cost, which dental or vision simply doesn't have.

Q: I couldn't see myself living in a RV if that's what it takes.
A: We pay $475/month to live here or $5700 per year. I budget for half of that which means in my budget, I count it as 475/2 =

$237.5/month. Note that $5700/year with, say, 1/3 paid in property taxes and maintenance would make for a mortgage payment of $3800/year, which at a 4% yield would correspond to a house of around $100,000. This will get you a shed (or an RV parking space) in California but a middle of the range house (2 bathrooms, 3 bed rooms, 1 garage) in many parts of the country. So no, you don't have to live in an RV although it's quite fun.

Q: I bet it's really cold/hot in the RV during winter/summer.
A: I hate to point out the obvious, but that depends on where you live! We live in the bay area which has a balmy climate almost all year around. Obviously, if we lived in cold Alaska, we'd buy a house instead. For year round living in an RV with low utility bills (we pay about $30/month for electricity or gas respectively), you should probably stick to a latitude of approximately 45 degrees.

Q: What about children? Do you plan to have them?
A: I have heard everything from how children lead to a fulfilling life to the opinion that life without children is meaningless. Now, I am the older sibling and when I was a kid my mother was running daycare for another kid eight years younger than me. In addition, my xGF had two teenagers. I have thus seen all aspects of parenthood from the first step and the first word to helping with homework and to be honest, my preferred ideal of having kids would be if they were 20 years old and moved out already Yes, it may be that there is a difference if they shared my own genetic material, but I don't think so.

Q: How can someone with children retire early?
A: The same way as people without children. By themselves, children actually spend very little money. The problem is parents spending money on their children without limits. If you adopt the same basic guidelines for your children as you do for yourself, the cost will be low. The fiscal or frugal problem happens when parents are willing to spend less on themselves but still create a consumer lifestyle for their children. I believe this is doing the children a disfavor. Unlike

stuff which you can just put in your garage, children need attention which you can either provide yourself or pay someone else to provide for you. Early retirement is a great way to provide time and attention and if you're smart you will wait the 5 years it takes to save enough money to be financially independent before having children.

Q: What about DW? How does she feel about work?
A: Like most people, DW does not consider her going to work for 8-10 hours a day as big a sacrifice as I do. Although it is impossible to predict how you feel about work down the line (The "I can see myself passionately working in my career until I die" statement is usually made by people with only a couple of years of working experience. I know. I used to say the very same thing.) she may be working until her ~~late 50s~~mid 40s or | so.

Q: How much did you make while working?
A: While I was in grad school, I earned Swiss Francs and the exchange rate is kind of lost in the fog of memory. Figure something like $20-25,000/year after tax. In my 5 years as a postdoc in the US, I earned $40,000, $41,000, $42,000, $67,000, and $69,000/year before tax. You can earn this kind of salary as a toll booth operator, a delivery truck driver, or a with a useful college degree. From a financial standpoint I was dumb enough to make it using a PhD and working in academia/government which is probably the most inefficient way to make money; but the work was interesting to me at the time.

Q: How can you retire on less than a million dollars?
A: The great majority of people never manage to accumulate a million dollars and so not that many actually retire on a million dollars. A million dollars is simply what is required to replace the expenses of an average consumer family, that is, about $50,000/year. Now obviously many families live in less than that. Consequently, they need less retirement funds. Conversely, some people cannot live on less than $100,000. I can't even imagine how someone is able to spend that much

money—if you gave me 100k and told me to spend it within a year, I'd probably still have 90k left by December despite trying very hard to waste it—but these families would need at least 2 million to retire.

Q: How do you deal with all your sacrifices?
A: How do you deal with yours? A sacrifice does not mean giving up something. A sacrifice means exchanging something for something better. I have given up shopping, credit cards, expensive cars, large houses, season tickets, and vacations in exchange for the joy of not having to work, the ability to spend all my time as I want, and the lack of stress from never having to struggle to make ends meet. If you know the answer to how you can sacrifice 60 hours of your life a week for the next 40 years, you know the answer to how I can sacrifice not eating out or buying stuff without thinking about the cost.

Q: How much did you pay for that? [Most common question IRL]
A: Probably nothing, unless it looks expensive in which case, probably more than you think. I buy luxury items from the "upper class" used (and so do they) and swap and recycle items with the "middle class" for free. You'll rarely see me in the mall.

Q: [Related] how can you live comfortably on so little money?
A: First, I spend my money more than twice as efficiently as the average person. This means I get more utility out of each dollar. Second, don't confuse spending money with living comfortably or having fun. Comfort is mainly about living without constant stress and fun is mainly about what you do rather than what you spend. If you can't do anything without spending, naturally you wouldn't have fun and you would probably also be stressed due to this inability. However, it is possible to overcome this inability. Third, when I buy things, I consider the long run. How much I pay for something now does not matter as much as how much it costs in the long run. I consider most of my purchases the way a business would.

Q: But with your degree you could earn so much more money…

A: Indeed, and if you increased the frequency of your breathing, you could gulp up so much more oxygen. But you don't because you have all the oxygen you need. Similarly, I have all the money I need. My goal in life is not to spend more money. To put it very simplistically, my goal is to become a more well-rounded and capable human. I strive for competence or personal growth if you will. More money will not help me do that. To give an example, no matter how much money you have or spend, you can't buy a black belt in martial arts. A black belt has to be earned with something other than money. So it is with many other things in life that cannot be bought, like friendship, respect, understanding, health, … When I was younger, I did indeed get a kick out of buying things, but it was a short lived joy. I found no long-term satisfaction in buying things. If buying stuff is enough to make you happy, then good for you.

Q: How can you be retired if you still make money? (Definitions of retirement, financial independence, and semi-retirement)

A: People used to work in one vocation until they grew old, worn down and nonproductive. Then they would be retired, "put out to pasture" so to speak, and get a pension. ERE shares some of these qualities but not all of them. Different generations have different definitions of what retirement means to them. The confusing part is that we use the same words to describe different things because ERE is still so uncommon that no common words exist. First, the concept of working only one career is outdated. Second, not many will be lucky enough to receive a pension. The point of ERE is to reach financial independence (FI). FI means having enough investments to pay all your expenses for the rest of your life WITHOUT needing to work. If you think of this as saving enough money to start your own trust fund, stipend, or a big annuity for yourself, you got it. (Many people who pursue ERE manage their own funds). Being freed from having to work to pay the bills, many EREs [plan to] retire from professional life in the sense of no longer working in that career. (For example, I was a physicist, but I no longer do any physics, I don't even think about it). This usually means taking up some other activity that is more meaningful to them but which would be hard to make a living from such as raising children, saving the world, rock climbing, making art, open source programming, writing, etc. It doesn't mean doing nothing. In that regard, some people say that I still work because I have this website. If you want to call that work, fine. Whatever rocks your boat. I call it a hobby and so does the IRS (I pay income taxes on my writing, but I don't take any deductions). I have no idea how much "work" I put into it. Sometimes 10 minutes per day, sometimes 50 minutes (if there's a particularly interesting forum discussion), some days none at all. But then every few months I spend a week hammering out a longer article for some magazine on a pro bono basis. Work work work ;-P

PS: To add to the confusion, "semi-retirement" is sometimes used to describe a person who derives some income from investments but not enough and thus needs a job, typically part-time, to make ends meet.

Q: You cannot be retired if your spouse is still working.
A: Why not? Is there a rule that states that either both must be working or both must be retired? I suspect part of the confusion comes about because married couples used to run all their finances jointly. This made sense when there was only one income earner. In our case there were two and we entered marriage with very different levels of wealth. In addition we had different goals. Therefore we kept our finances separate. This avoids a lot of arguments about whether or not to spend on something. We only need to agree on things we buy "for the house" and are free to buy things for ourselves without consulting the spouse.

Q: You're not retired. You're just a stay at home spouse.
A: The difference between a stay at home spouse and me is that I am independently wealthy and don't need my spouse's income/handouts. In other words, I am not a "dependent". I pay half of the household expenses with investment income

from money I saved and my wife pays the other half with money she earns from working.

Q: Isn't your low budget predicated on you being married and sharing expenses?
A: No. I do not spend less money now compared to when I was single. Our budget is a compromise. We share expenses 50/50 for household expenses but not personal entertainment, personal savings, or personal health care. If we got divorced, I would no longer be paying half of some of these expenses, like the car, and food and heating would also be lower. Conversely, I might be paying more in housing unless I could find a roommate or something similar like subletting parts of the house/apartment.

Q: This may work for you, but it would never work for me.
A: Is this your problem or mine? Regardless, don't get too involved in copying what I do. I primarily write with the intention of providing guidelines rather than plans. I show you that this could work and give you one specific example of how I made it work. I know there are a few other bloggers who work along similar lines and they do things slightly different from me. What we all have in common are really high savings rates and rather low levels of expenses which in monetary terms would be considered poverty levels or at least be much lower than the money we would be expected to spend to keep up [in the spending competition] without incomes. We differ in terms of how we invest e.g. stocks, real estate, or private businesses or how we manage not to pay for things e.g. repairing things, being minimalists, work camping, or homesteading.

Q: You're not retired, you're a blogger, and based on your Alexa/google/etc. ranking you're making $120,000 per year
A: Ha! You wouldn't happen to be one of those who lost a bundle in similar optimistic valuations during the dot com bubble? Let me tell you what, you give me $100,000 and you can take over my blog. If you're right you should recoup your investment in 10 months. That's a great deal if you're right.

But you're wrong. A well-monetized personal finance blog can make $3-8eCPM, that's 3–8 bucks for per 1000 views. You can see how many views ERE gets by checking my sitemeter stats. Even if I really put my back into it, I'd still make less than $1000/month (*). Actually, I make more like ~~$100~~$200/month on ads. My rates are given here and here. Now multiply by the number of ads I'm running and subtract a 25% administrative fee. Sure, I'm probably leaving money on the table and, sure, I could earn more if I did more SEO, inserted more payday loan and mortgage text links, and sold affiliate junk. ~~Note that I also makes about 6-7% for anything sold through amazon.com. This varies from $30-200 per month. It's usually around $100. The way it works is that amazon leaves a cookie on your machine if you click on a link; then I get my cut from anything you buy within the next 24 hours—people rarely buy what I talk about on the blog, it's usually something else. Thanks to the new California nexus law, Amazon terminated its contract with all its California affiliates. Thus I no longer make any money through the Amazon program. Apparently the government of California realized that their nexus law had unintended consequences (such as a massive loss of taxable small business income) and they have reverted their decision, at least for another year. I'm now again an amazon affiliate.~~ I am once again NOT an Amazon affiliate because I now live in Illinois which takes the same stance that California used to take.

(*) This would, however, be more than enough for me to live on. Yet I don't recommend making your living as a blogger. The pressure to perform is very high and writing for a living can easily lead to burnout. If you don't believe me and you haven't been blogging for more than a couple of years, please wait and check back with me in a few years before you disagree

Q: If you're financially independent, why does your book cost money?
A: If I may paraphrase Andre Kostolany (a famous and wealthy stock market speculator): "When people buy my book, the fact that I receive the proceeds of the sale is secondary (*)

to the fact that people are willing to pay money to read my ideas." Yes, it's a vanity thing. If the book was free, sure, maybe tens of thousands would download it, but I would have no idea whether they valued it. They might not even read it. Most CEOs, actors, rock stars, famous writers, billionaires, etc. do it. Why shouldn't I?

(*) Overall, my book sales have increased my net worth by 7%. If I had wanted to increase my wealth, there are far better ways of doing so that writing. A minimum wage job would have been a much more profitable use of my time.

Q: Why don't you donate the proceeds/your money to charity?
A: For the same reasons that Warren Buffett held on to his money. In my case, I think I can do more good (judging by the number of nice emails and comments I receive) in the long run by using the money to support my own work on ERE than donating it to nonprofit groups where I fear it would just be eaten up by administrative salaries and other inefficiencies. Ultimately I do intend to get rid of all of it before I die but it will require years to find a good cause that's run equally efficient.

Q: Would you like to be on my radio program/TV show/national newspaper?
A: I used to respond positively to these request but after seeing the typical popular reaction, my answer is now no. Mass media in its current form is unfortunately an unsuitable format for presenting ideas that are controversial and complex in nature.

Q: Why did you take a job and go back to work?
A: Just as there were several reasons that I decide to retire from physics and spend my time writing ERE (lost interest in physics, didn't like the politics required for an academic career, felt that writing about ERE was more important, ...) there were several reasons why I decided to take this job and go forward to work. First, I felt like had exhausted everything there was to say (at least on a daily basis) about ERE. I don't feel like repeating myself and thus the blog has been on autopilot since fall 2010. Second, the personal cost to me and

my family from slanderous attacks from random people who haven't read or understood much of the site but felt like giving their opinion anyway was beginning to take too much of my energy as the blog was getting more and more popular. Everybody has a tolerance limit for this and I was reaching mine. It's not really fun being a public figure associated with controversial subjects like saving money and not being a consumer when some show little restraint in terms of quoting out of context, making things up, and/or using asinine sensationalism to make their point. I guess it's similar to being a politician and dealing with attack ads, only in my case the attacks mainly show up on various forums on the internet. Third, working in finance has been on my "bucket list" for several years. I always thought it would be a cool thing to try working with one of the world's primary information systems that decides how the world runs (the three systems are politics, economics, and ecology), so when this opportunity was offered to me through a friend of mine the decision was easy to make.

Understanding things in their proper "historic" context, it was clear, if not to me, then to many of my long-term readers, that my enthusiasm for the blog had been fading for quite a while already and that I was ready to move on to something new. Until this offer came along it was not entirely clear what it was going to be yet. I had been talking about touring across the US on a bike OR building a tiny house OR even buying an RV park to create a kind of ERE city full of like-minded people. But seeing this was a once in a lifetime offer (at least as far as I'm concerned) I had to say yes or probably regret it later.

If that confused a few people's definition of "retirement", so be it …

In general this decision was entirely consistent with what I have been writing about all along: Always further a broad set of valuable skills (the Renaissance ideal) and arrange your finances (financial independence) and lifestyle (self-reliance and location/independence) in a way that increases your resilience and the number of opportunities you have in life. Did I forget anything?

The Wheaton Eco Scale
Paul Wheaton
Posted Wednesday, February 03, 2010 11:41:18 AM

http://www.permies.com/t/3069/toxin-ectomy/Wheaton-Eco-Scale

The time has come for me to more formally define this. I have alluded to this rough idea in the past with some numbers I pulled out of my butt. I now flush those numbers and clearly define these new numbers.

Further, while in the shower this morning, I decided that I am obnoxious and arrogant enough to come up with something and put my name to it. I also give everybody else license to come up with their own scales for whatever they want. I just need to express myself, so I need ...SOMETHING!

Wheaton eco level 0: about 5 billion people
Wheaton eco level 1: about a billion people
Wheaton eco level 2: about 100 million people
Wheaton eco level 3: about 10 million people
Wheaton eco level 4: about a million people
Wheaton eco level 5: about 100,000 people
Wheaton eco level 6: about 10,000 people
Wheaton eco level 7: about a thousand people
Wheaton eco level 8: about 100 people
Wheaton eco level 9: about 10 people
Wheaton eco level 10: Sepp Holzer

Observation 1: most people find folks one or two levels up took pretty cool. People three levels up look a bit nutty. People four of five levels up look downright crazy. People six levels up should probably be institutionalized. I find the latter reactions to be inappropriate.

Observations 2: most people find that folks one level back are ignorant. Two levels back are assholes. Any further back and they should be shot on sight for the betterment of society as a whole. I find that all of these reactions are inappropriate.

Finally: I can put whoever I want at the spot of eco level 10. I choose the mighty Sepp Holzer and I don't give a damn if you think somebody else should sit in that spot on my scale!

Here are some possible attributes of people on the scale

Level 1: is thinking about the environment. Bought fluorescent light bulbs. Is trying to do a good job of recycling. Reads an article or two. Buys some organic food. Their power bill is less than average.

Level 2: 30% of purchased food is organic

Level 3: Has an organic garden and 80% of purchased food is organic

Level 4: Grow 40% of their own food. Studying permaculture. **Got rid of all fluorescent light bulbs**

Level 5: has taken a PDC and/or grows 90% of their own food

Level 6: Living a footprint that is 10 times lighter than average. Maybe living in community. Maybe living in something very small.

Level 7: Permaculture teacher

Level 8: Doing things that are currently improving the world in big ways

Level 9: masanobu fukuoka, Paul Stamets, Art Ludwig, Bill Mollison, and Ianto Evans....

Level 10: the mighty, the glorious, the amazing Sepp Holzer

Chapter 4 – How to Find Cheap Health Insurance

http://earlyretirementextreme.com/ere-health-insurance.html

Health insurance for extreme early retirement
Published on March 30th, 2012
Posted by Jacob in Health

These days not too many people get their health insurance on the free market. Instead many have no coverage at all and many get it through their employer where it acts as a set of golden handcuffs, that is, the only thing preventing some people from quitting their jobs. Indeed, some still have a job simply in order to have access to affordable health care.

(Note, of all the developed countries in the world, this peculiar problem only pertains to the US, so if you live somewhere else, you can ignore this post.)

However, it is possible to get health insurance on the free market and it does offer a greater flexibility than "corporate health care" (*). Even when I had access to "good benefits" through my W-2 job, I elected to go with the "free market insurance" instead. In fact, even after I had retired from my career/job/employee-status and I could come in under DW's plan; I stayed with my own plan.

(*) A kind of socialized health care available to people who are W-2 employees of tax-subsidized corporations.

I currently (2011) pay $91/month for a $4500 deductible HSA-compatible plan with HealthNet.

I consider $91/month a small sum. It is certainly nothing that's going to break my retirement plans. Indeed, these plans exist even as people tell me they are spending hundreds, some close to a thousand each month for fully loaded health plans; and that would be something that would break ERE.

To verify my numbers, go to ehealthinsurance.com and enter my zip code (94551) and county (Alameda) and my age (I'm 35.5ish). It'll give you a long list of plans. Go to the bottom in the left sidebar and click on Additional Features. Click on HSA-eligible. Then sort by price.

Note that the cheapest one comes in at $81/month.

Maybe I should change my plan.

Next, let's see what the plan will cost in 20 years in today's dollars (presuming business as usual and no fix to the most expensive health care system in the world), when I'm 55. Repeating the exercise, the cost would be $245/month. I also ran the plan for age 60 and it came to $288/month.

Shortly after that evil socialized health care, you know, Medicare will be available to my age group.

Again, none of these amounts are restrictive for ERE. At that age, it's very likely safe to move from the ultra safe 3% withdrawal rate to a standard 4% withdrawal rate.

Now, I know that some areas/states are more expensive and some are cheaper. This is due to various regulations based on how much the insurance company can discriminate against things like gender, pre-existing conditions, smokers, obesity, etc. For instance, my premiums recently went up thanks to some California program that's intended to provide cheaper health care for most people [which in turn means that some people, like me, are left holding the bag.] If you live in an extremely expensive state, consider moving. I promise you, if my premium costs were $500/month compared to $100/month in some other state, I'd be out of California within a month.

Of course, there's still the question of the high deductible. The answer is that your HSA covers you. I'm adding $3050 to my HSA every year. This means it takes me 3 years to cover my deductible for two years. If I break my leg, I can take this out of the HSA. I just need to make sure that I don't break a limb more than once every 1.5 years. If I stay healthy, the HSA works like an IRA. Should some situation arise where I need to spend down my entire deductible year after year, I would presume that the situation is terminal and I might as well start spending down my six-figure ERE investment principal. This would still take decades.

Of course, part of my plan is also to stay healthy and not rely on modern medicine to compensate for bad personal habits. Poor lifestyle choices account for 50-75% of all health care costs. Fortunately, ERE is not a poor lifestyle: no driving, no stress, and no eating out.

This still leaves the 25%-50% of the rest of the costs, most of which is simply old age cost, that is, trying to keep a geriatric alive for a few more months (on average, some live much longer, but most don't), but some of which are driven by genetic factors, like type I diabetes and other inherited diseases. Unfortunately, I don't have an ERE solution for this (beyond leaving the US for another developed country, like Mexico). This is a problem better fixed by your political representative.

Chapter 5 – More on HDHP HAS Health Insurance

http://earlyretirementextreme.com/my-hdhp-hsa-and-some-comments-on-health-care.html

My HDHP HSA and some comments on health care
Published on August 20th, 2012
Posted by Jacob in Health, How to

I must be crazy. I ~~have~~had a government job and thus the best |
health insurance in the world at a very low cost and yet I
cancelled my plan and went with a private provider, why?

First of all, I think relying on an employer for health care is
positively evil and that this practice should end ASAP by
removing all corporate tax incentives and other incentives to
offer it to their employees. I prefer to walk my talk rather than
just talk.
Second of all, I think that relying on a medical doctor to remain
healthy is positively backwards. While I would certainly
welcome the assistance of a doctor to reset a bone or perform
surgery, my faith in medical doctors does not go much beyond
this (*). I prefer a proactive approach to health rather than a
reactive approach.

(*) I think this is because having a somewhat longer and somewhat more difficult education compared to an MD and being all too aware of how little I actually know, it is hard to be impressed. The main benefit of a doctor is the comfort of thinking that you're dealing with an expert. If you don't believe that, much of the magic goes away. Why do you think doctors wear white coats? Why does a magician wear a black top hat and wave a wand? Indeed!

Furthermore I am not willing to pay for the philosophy that drives US health care (click on the link above and read the comments to see my opinion on that) which seems to focus on pharmaceuticals rather than lifestyle. In that regard a very interesting quantity is the numbers needed to treat. This number reflects the marginal utility of a treatment, e.g. how many people do we need to treat to prevent ONE ADDITIONAL BAD OUTCOME. This number can be on the order of a hundred or more. This means that you need to put 100 people on medication to save 1 person. Is it worth it? That depends on the side effects which are measured in a similar way called number needed to harm. Suppose a drug has an NNT of 100 and a NNH of 5, would you take it? It means that it would save 1 in 100 people but harm 20 in the process 19 of which would otherwise not have had to suffer.

Of course this depends on exactly what the treatment prevents and how it harms, but I don't think that there is any arguing that compared to other countries, which have equally life spans yet pay half for their health care, US health care is an expensive drag on the system.

Yes, in the US you get to watch a movie on an LCD screen while the dentist is drilling, but seriously … I don't want to pay extra for that.

The way to minimize the drag is to become proactive with your health — There's little reason not to as you practically ARE your health — and wrestle back control of your health insurance.

I went to ~~hsainsider.com~~ ehealthinsurance.com and after 10 minutes found a high deductible health plan (HDHP) with a $3500 deductible. This plan provides pretty much the same benefits as big low deductible group plans except that I pay the first $3500 out of pocket. This protects me from catastrophic incidents. I pay $72 each month. I am a 33 year old male with no history other than allergies which I am practically free from due to behavioral modifications over the past 30 years. I'm just mentioning this because I know that there are going to be non-believers stating that it is impossible to get away with paying $72 a month.

Now, it actually turns out that it is less than that thanks to the health savings account. Read more about HSAs below. I have not established one yet, but I'm thinking of going with Wells Fargo. I can put in $3000 in 2009. This is fully tax deductible and since we're in the 25% bracket, this reduces our taxes by $750. There is a maintenance fee of $4.25/month, so 750-12*4.25=$699. My premiums are $864 for a year. This means I'm paying $165 for a year or $13.75 a month on health insurance. Not bad!

Update: I have now established the HSA mentioned above.

Not the $3000 can be invested inside the HSA. If I do not incur any health care costs over the first year and get 5% ROI, that's $150, which makes my monthly health insurance come in slight over one dollar! If I go on for a second year (for the record it's been about 6 years since I last saw a doctor), I will actually see positive return.

If I keep up the 90% clean lifestyle, I do believe I have the ideal setup. Once I hit old age, the HSA can even be converted into something IRA like (I have not checked out the details) which frees the money for things other than pure health related expenses.

15 Things you should know about HSAs

Published on April 17th, 2011
Posted by Jacob in Finance, Health

http://earlyretirementextreme.com/15-things-you-should-know-about-hsas.html

This is a guest post from Joel, who is a CFP® and a serial entrepreneur who loves working on various Internet based projects. Some of his most recent ventures include various consumer comparison financial websites including websites for finding life insurance http://www.insuranceproviders.com/life-insurance/, comparing car insurance companies http://www.carinsurancecomparison.com/car-insurance-companies/, and researching credit card offers http://www.creditcardchaser.com/. He is a newcomer to Early Retirement Extreme and one of his favorite posts is on ERE is "My 4 Hour Work Week".

With all of the upcoming changes that will be coming down the pike due to the health care reform bill there seems to be an ever increasing desire to understand a type of health insurance option that has risen in popularity in recent years: the Health Savings Account (HSA). I personally have had an HSA for the last 4 years and I couldn't be happier with my United Healthcare HSA 100 Plan. Additionally, Jacob mentions in the FAQ section of the site that he utilizes an HSA as well. Aside from my personal satisfaction and apparently Jacob's satisfaction as well in having chosen a Health Savings Account I think that there are a multitude of reasons why an HSA could be a great choice for just about anyone. Here are 15 things that you should know about HSA's before making a decision for or against an HSA.

#1 An HSA is NOT a Health Insurance Plan
"What!?! An HSA is not health insurance? What are you talking about?" Let me explain. A Health Savings Account is just that: a savings account. You can set up this special type of savings account at almost any bank and you can deposit

money just like you would into a plain vanilla savings account (some HSA's also allow stocks, bonds, and other investments). Technically, an HSA is just a savings account but practically speaking many people refer to their high deductible health insurance plans (HDHP) that are required in order to set up an HSA as an "HSA health insurance plan". However, you should most certainly understand that an HSA is in fact made up of 2 different components: the health insurance component (i.e. the HDHP) and the savings account component (i.e. the HSA).

#2 Money Contributed to an HSA Gives You an "Above the Line" Tax Deduction

It's pretty easy to load up on itemized deductions when doing tax planning. Charitable contributions, mortgage interest paid, health care costs, and many other things can all be taken as an itemized deduction. However, all money that you contribute into an HSA (up to certain IRS annual limits) is eligible for an "above the line" deduction. An above the line deduction is a deduction that is taken on the front of your 1040 tax return before calculating your Adjusted Gross Income (AGI) and is therefore much more valuable than an itemized deduction. In addition to being an above the line deduction, all HSA contributions are free from any income phaseouts. You could be Bill Gates and still take a deduction for HSA contributions. The higher your tax bracket then the more valuable this HSA contribution deduction becomes.

#3 Money Inside of an HSA Grows Tax Free

You are no doubt familiar with the important difference between tax free growth and tax deferred growth as it is illustrated quite nicely with the popular retirement plans the Roth IRA (and example of the former) and the Traditional IRA (an example of the latter). As long as you use the money in your HSA for qualified medical expenses (or for your retirement once you reach the age of 65) then the money in your HSA will grow tax free and NOT just tax deferred.

#4 Money Inside of an HSA Rolls Over from Year to Year

Many people mistakenly assume that Health Savings Accounts are exactly the same as a Flexible Spending Account in that the money must be used up every year ("use it or lose it"). While this is certainly true of Flexible Spending Accounts the great thing about money contributed to an HSA is that the money rolls over from year to year and continues to build – and hey, if you don't end up using all of the money in your HSA for medical expenses by the time you are age 65 then that is a good thing for two reasons: A) You didn't have a lot of medical expenses and B) You can now use the money in your HSA that has been growing tax free for your retirement.

#5 When You Change Your Health Plan You Don't Have to Change Your HSA

Another common assumption about HSA's is that once you sign up for an HSA that if you ever want to find a new health insurance plan that you will then have to shut down your HSA as well. This is not true. Since an HSA is simply the savings account component of the mix then you are free at any time to change health insurance companies and purchase a new health plan while still maintaining your HSA at your current bank. Of course, your new health insurance plan must still meet the IRS requirements for a high deductible plan although you are free to switch to any company you like (and in fact shopping around and comparing health insurance plans at least once per year is a smart way to make sure that you always have the best plan for the lowest rate as rates can change often).

#6 High Deductibles are NOT Really that High

Many people are scared off by the term high deductible health insurance plan. An HSA sounds great in theory but for some it can be very hard to switch from the copay plans that they have had for all of their adult lives to a high deductible plan with no co-pays. The current IRS definition of a high deductible health insurance plan for 2010 (the limits change every year as they are indexed for inflation) is a deductible of no lower than $1,200 for an individual and $2,400 for a family.

Sure, if you purchase an HSA and the next month you get hit with a huge medical bill then you likely may feel the pain of having to shell out $1,200 if you have an individual plan or $2,400 for a family plan to meet your deductible but if you can make it through the first year and at least max out your HSA contribution for the first year then from years 2 and on you have money just sitting in your HSA waiting for you to use it to pay towards your deductible as soon as you need it – and growing tax free at that!

#7 Your Out of Pocket Expense is Limited by Law

Another thing that scares many people with a HDHP is that they think that their potential for paying for their health care costs extends virtually forever. However, in all HSA compatible health plans must adhere to certain maximum out of pocket cost limitations imposed by the IRS. For 2010 those out of pocket limitation are $5,950 for individuals and $11,900 for families. Also, the more that consumers are forced to pay for their health care out of their own pocket (at least initially until the insurance kicks in) then the more price conscious we will all become which will in turn drive down health care costs across the board (and hey – a side benefit is that we might even start to pay attention to things like our BMI, our VO2 Max, eating healthy, etc. as we will start to realize a direct cause and effect relationship between our health and our pocket books).

#8 Many Companies Offer HSA Compatible Plans

If you want a Humana plan then they have an HSA. If you want a United Healthcare plan then they have an HSA. If you want a Blue Cross Blue Shield plan then they have an HSA. If you want an Aetna plan then they have an HSA. If you – well you get the picture.

#9 HSA Money can be Invested Just Like an IRA

Anything that is eligible for investment into an IRA can be invested into an HSA. Of course, different HSA trustees at different banks may have their own internal regulations but according to the IRS: stocks, bonds, mutual funds, and CD's are all fair game.

#10 Your HSA Money Does Not Disappear When You Die
While many are rightfully very cynical of Uncle Sam at times it is not true that when an HSA account holder dies that Uncle Sam is standing right next to the Grim Reaper ready to snatch the money out of your HSA account. HSA accounts can have beneficiaries just like any other account and the money is paid out to your beneficiary when you die or to your estate if there is no beneficiary.

#11 You Can Roll Over Money from an IRA into an HAS
Since 2007 the IRS has allowed a special one-time rollover from an IRA directly to an HSA. This special rollover is not eligible for 401k's or other retirement plans but IRA's are allowed this special tax treatment on a one time basis.

#12 Employers Can Contribute to an HSA for an Employee
Employers can make HSA contributions on behalf of their employees. Employers can make as much or as little of a contribution as they like (while staying within the annual IRS contribution limits). There is no vesting schedule for HSA contributions. Employees own 100% of the money in their HSA at all times regardless of whether it is an employer or employee contributed amount.

#13 Paying for Medical Expenses from an HSA is Easy
Paying for medical expenses from an HSA is as easy as swiping a credit card, debit card, or writing a check. Almost all Health Savings Accounts come with debit cards and check writing privileges.

#14 Self Employed People Should Love HSA's
When you couple the self employed health insurance premiums paid tax deduction with the HSA contribution tax deduction then you have two great above the line tax deductions that those who are self employed should try their very best to take advantage of – especially when you consider

the fact that you can take both of these deductions together and there are no income phase outs (although you can't use the self employed health insurance tax deduction to give your business a loss).

#15 What About YOU?
What did I miss? What other things do you like about HSA's or feel are important things to know about HSA's?

Chapter 6 – You Can Do it!

As a behavioral scientist, I filter everything through systematic science. I try to look at things through all angles such as social, fiscal, etc. Retirement is on a good many people's mind today because of the economic downturn in our economy is affecting the ability to retire. A good many nest eggs have been wiped out. Many people relied completely on the equity in their homes to be the main contributing factor to their nest eggs and not only is this no longer viable; many are upside down in their mortgages. In other words, options are disappearing and there is a lot of pain and fear out there.

Let's now discuss the behavioral science aspects as to what is happening out there. In systematic science, a theory is first proposed and when the theory cannot be disproved (we call this falsification) then it becomes a law of science.

In the early 1900s, Einstein proposed the theory of relativity ($e=mc^2$). In 1933, this theory became the law of relativity because no one could disprove it.

I mention this fact for a reason; in psychology and behavioral science too, there are no laws; only theories. As a behavioral scientist, my colleagues and I attempt falsification of the many theories proposed over the 150 year history of psychology but so far this has not occurred. The most famous theory of psychology is called "cognitive dissonance" and it was proposed by Leon Festinger in 1957. Basically stated, cognitive dissonance is defined as "actions inconsistent with beliefs.

The human mind is made up of the conscious mind and the subconscious mind. The conscious mind takes everything in through the five senses and sees reality for what it is. The conscious mind "reacts" to this reality.

The subconscious mind is made up of the intellect – both empirical and experiential and the desires, emotions and will of an individual. It perceives the reality that the conscious mind sees and this perception can be different than the reality itself. The subconscious mind interacts with the perceived reality. All behavior/conduct/action comes from the subconscious mind and is a result of a belief system acted upon by thought using either the intellect or the desires, emotions and will.

Fear is a conscious mind reaction. Let me give you an example. If I were to throw a ball at your head, your conscious mind would "react' by bring your arm up to block the ball. Your subconscious mind would "interact" by seeing me as a future threat to your well being and when we meet again it would do everything to avoid me.

The subconscious mind is also responsible for goals. Early retirement is a goal but is it a good goal or a bad goal? Let's see…

Which of the following goals are good goals?

❖ To want to get married and have a wonderful, happy, loving marriage?
❖ To want to have children who are happy, successful, and loving?
❖ To have a successful, fulfilling and rewarding career?

❖ Is it a good goal to want to have fun, bonded, loving, and meaningful relationships with other people?

Which of the listed goals are good goals? None of them!

You should never have anything for a goal that is not 100% under your control, AND each and every goal should be motivated by love.

Almost all goals that we have in our life are wrong.

Everything that we do, we do because of a goal we have.

When we get up in the morning, it's because of some goal that we have; we are hungry for breakfast, or we need to go to work.

If we go to the grocery store, it's because of some goal we have. If we are kind to people, it's because of some goal that we have.

Now we don't always know what they are, because a lot of these are subconscious goals.

The goals we have are the reasons for everything we do. But, do all of your goals involve only YOU?

Of course not!

And when the other person, or persons, in your goal do not perform, or act the way you want them to, then we become anxious and stressed.

When our goals get blocked, it creates anger, anxiety, and frustration. If we only have good goals, we will not experience anger or anxiety.

That's how you know, if you are living a wrongful goal. If the result is anger and frustration because your control was blocked and blocking your goal, then you had a wrongful goal.

It may have been a fine and noble desire, but a wrongful goal.

So, is early retirement a good goal or a bad goal? Is it motivated by love and a goal where you are completely in control?

After reading my definition of goals above many of you would answer that it is a bad goal and if you did answer this way then you are WRONG!

The entire purpose of this book is to demonstrate to you that early retirement with little or no money is an attainable goal where you are in control. Love is defined as sacrifice to attain any goal. You love your spouse, girlfriend pet and you are committed to their care and well being because you love them. The goal of early retirement is an act of love since in order to achieve this goal you must sacrifice.

This is evident in Jacob Fisker's words written above. People have developed a certain lifestyle (mindset) and are not willing to sacrifice and change their "reality' to attain early retirement.

But the fact remains that you can do it!

Sometimes I believe that everything would be okay if the New York press would go out of business. The media is responsible for the permeation of fear in our society coupled with government's inability to fix the fiscal dilemma.

Don't "react' to fear; "interact" with it and use it to motivate yourself to make the lifestyle changes necessary now while you still can. Begin to downsize and cut your monthly budgets. Get rid of things you don't need.

Personally I had four big storage units of 'stuff" that I had accumulated over the years. I called up my children and told them to take what they wanted because I was going to sell everything else and I did. Paying a monthly fee for four big storage units was just plain dumb. I have now gotten rid of that bill and made a tidy fortune selling off everything that was in storage. And my kids are happy because they got a bunch of neat stuff.

I have to tell you that I was very amazed when I looked at my personal budget and determined that I could cut a ton of monthly overhead from it easily. You can too when you study your own budgets and begin to downsize.

One of my main goals is to pay off everything and live debt free. I do not have a lot of personal debt so this isn't going to be a painful experience for me like some of you might have. My two main assets – home and car - are already paid for and this isn't the case with most people. My point is to put in place a plan and stick to it. Begin to downsize now in all areas of your lifestyle. You will find that it is actually quite refreshing having the debt burdens removed from your life.

You Can Do It! This is not a flippant remark either. You will be totally amazed at what you are capable of doing when you have the proper mindset and goal. I see this fact every day. Can you do everything written here? No but you can do many of them. Do the ones that fit your lifestyle.

I have lived my life by one main credo and this is it: "I don't want you to do your best. Doing your best is the Devil's lie and gives you an excuse to blame when you fail. I WANT YOU TO DO WHAT IS REQUIRED!"

When I was a boy growing up my father never allowed any excuses. He demanded I do what was required. This credo has never failed me; I never allow myself the luxury of saying I did my best. Do what is required and you will literally be stunned at your success.

Blessings to you all.

I Have a Special Gift for My Readers

I appreciate my readers for without them I am just another struggling author attempting to make ends meet.

My readers and I have in common a passion for the written word as well as the desire to learn and grow from books.

My special offer to you is a massive ebook library that I have compiled over the years. It contains hundreds of fiction and non-fiction ebooks in Adobe Acrobat PDF format as well as the Greek classics and old literary classics too.

In fact, this library is so massive to completely download the entire library will require over 5 GBs open on your desktop.

Use the link below and scan all of the ebooks in the library. You can select the ebooks you want individually or download the entire library.

The link below does not expire after a given time period so you are free to return for more books rather than clog your desktop. And feel free to give the link to your friends who enjoy reading too.

I thank you for reading my book and hope if you are pleased that you will leave me an honest review so that I can improve my work and or write books that appeal to your interests.

Okay, here is the link…

http://tinyurl.com/special-readers-promo

PS: If you wish to reach me personally for any reason you may simply write to mailto:support@epubwealth.com.

I answer all of my emails so rest assured I will respond.

Meet the Author

Dr. Noah Pranksky is a research behavioral scientist for Applied Mind Sciences. His research involves many aspects of the human mind including relationships, energy psychology, and various protocols and modalities relating to treatment and cure of various mental maladies. He and his wife Marianne reside in Portland, Oregon.

www.ingramcontent.com/pod-product-compliance
Lightning Source LLC
Chambersburg PA
CBHW071630170526
45166CB00003B/1276